Everyday 3-D Shapes

Cylinders

by Laura Hamilton Waxman
illustrated by Kathryn Mitter

Content Consultant: Paula J. Maida, PhD
Department of Mathematics, Western Connecticut State University

magic
wagon

visit us at
www.abdopublishing.com

Published by Magic Wagon, a division of the ABDO Group, PO Box 398166,
Minneapolis, MN 55439. Copyright © 2013 by Abdo Consulting Group, Inc.
International copyrights reserved in all countries. All rights reserved. No part of
this book may be reproduced in any form without written permission from the
publisher.

Looking Glass Library™ is a trademark and logo of Magic Wagon.
Printed in the United States of America, North Mankato, Minnesota.
042012
092012

 THIS BOOK CONTAINS AT LEAST 10% RECYCLED MATERIALS.

Text by Laura Hamilton Waxman
Illustrations by Kathryn Mitter
Edited by Rebecca Felix
Series design by Craig Hinton

Library of Congress Cataloging-in-Publication Data
Waxman, Laura Hamilton.
Cylinders / by Laura Hamilton Waxman ; illustrated by Kathryn Mitter.
pages cm -- (Everyday 3-D Shapes)
Content Consultant: Dr. Paula Maida.
ISBN 978-1-61641-874-8
1. Cylinder (Mathematics)--Juvenile literature. 2. Shapes--Juvenile literature.
3. Geometry, Solid--Juvenile literature. I. Mitter, Kathy, illustrator. II. Title.
QA491.W375 2012
516'.156--dc23
2012007116

Tall or short, this shape curves round.

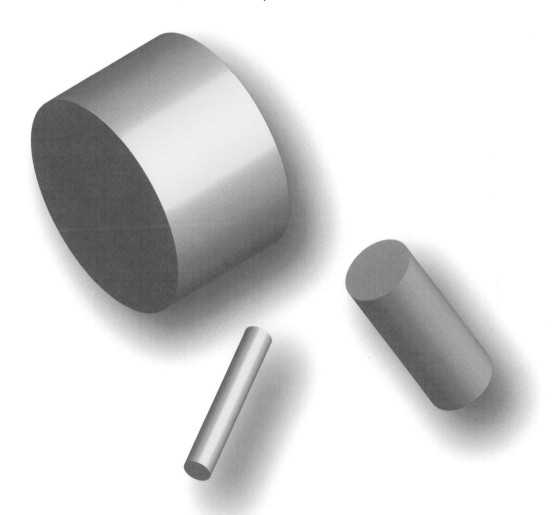

Where can cylinders be found?

4

The same size round base is on each end.

Cylinder sides are one curving bend.

Look around for this shape's look.

Search for cylinders in this book.

Ben sees cylinders in the store.

Tall stacks of cans are by the door.

Jill finds rolls of towels and tape.

Both things have a cylinder shape!

Cylinder of windows to the sky.

Cylinder poles reach just as high!

13

Ben likes to go down the cylinder slide.

In cylinder tunnels, Jill likes to hide.

15

Cows eat grass on the farm all day.

Sheep graze on cylinders of hay.

17

Here are cylinders on top of brooms.

Nice round handles for sweeping rooms.

Time for a snack and a nice cool drink.

White cylinder cheese and juice that's pink.

Cylinders aren't just in this book.

They're all around you. Take a look!

I Spy a Cylinder Game

Look around. Find a cylinder. Then say, "I spy a cylinder that is . . ." and name its color. Everyone has to guess what cylinder you see. Then it is someone else's turn to spy a cylinder. You can guess what it is.

Count the Cylinders Game

Choose a room in your home. Count how many cylinders you can find.

Words to Know

base: the bottom of something.

cylinder: a shape with the same sized round top and bottom and a curved side.

graze: to feed on grass or hay in a field.

round: something that is circular in shape and has an equal distance from the center to any part of the edge.

shape: the form or look something has.